NEW MEXICO

impressions

photography and text by **Laurence Parent**

FARCOUNTRY
PRESS

Right: Chimney Rock towers over Ghost Ranch. The ranch was made famous by the paintings of Georgia O'Keeffe, who lived on the ranch and painted it for many years. The Presbyterian Church now runs it as a retreat and conference center.

Far right: The Mogollon Range towers over the irrigated fields of the Gila River Valley. The mountains lie at the heart of the Gila Wilderness, the nation's first designated wilderness. The 558,000-acre wilderness is the largest in the Southwest.

Front cover: Rancho de las Golondrinas (Ranch of the Swallows) near Santa Fe was purchased by Miguel Vega y Coca in 1710 and operated as a ranch and stop on the Camino Real from Santa Fe to Mexico. Today it is preserved as a living-history museum with a house, mill, church, and defensive tower.

Back cover: In 1270 a small group of Mogollon people built cliff dwellings in a side canyon of the Gila River's West Fork. The buildings were abandoned in the early 1300s. The ruins lie within Gila Cliff Dwellings National Monument on the edge of the Gila Wilderness.

Title page: The sun sets over the Gila River Valley in southwestern New Mexico. The Gila has the longest stretch of undammed river in the Southwest.

ISBN 1-56037-312-1
Photography © 2004 Laurence Parent
© 2004 Farcountry Press
Text by Laurence Parent

For more information about our books write Farcountry Press, P.O. Box 5630, Helena, MT 59604; call (800) 821-3874; or visit www.farcountrypress.com.

Created, produced, and designed in the United States. Printed in China.

Left: The ruins of the mission church at Abó rise before the peaks of the Manzano Mountains. The Spaniards established the mission in 1622. It was abandoned in 1673 because of drought, famine, disease, and attacks by Apaches and Comanches.

Below: Petroglyphs decorate the rocks in the desert foothills of Cookes Peak in south-western New Mexico.

Right: Wheeler Peak, the state's highest point at 13,161 feet, rises above lush forests of aspen, spruce, fir, and pine. The peak and the surrounding high country are protected within the Wheeler Peak Wilderness. The wilderness adjoins Taos Ski Valley.

Below: A mule deer roams the slopes of Capulin Volcano. The deer are common throughout all parts of the state.

Left: During Feast Day in San Juan Pueblo, the largest of the Tewa-speaking pueblos, even the youngest of the tribe takes part in an age-old tradition. STEPHEN TRIMBLE

Far left: Sunset paints the sky over Black Canyon in the Guadalupe Mountains. The rugged mountains are a part of the Lincoln National Forest in southeastern New Mexico.

Below: The oldest members of the San Juan Pueblo celebrate Feast Days with bright attire and great hope for productive crops. STEPHEN TRIMBLE

Right: The Sandia Mountains tower more than a vertical mile over the Rio Grande in this view a short distance upstream from Albuquerque.

Below: A large field of weathered blocks of tuff make up City of Rocks State Park. The rock was deposited as ash from a volcanic eruption more than 30 million years ago. Hikers and climbers enjoy the unique formations.

Above: The Santuario de Guadalupe with its thick adobe walls was built in Santa Fe by Franciscans between 1776 and 1796. Over the years it has been renovated several times. Its current form is believed to match its original appearance.

Left: The Sandia Mountains rise abruptly from the east side of Albuquerque, reaching a height of 10,678 feet at Sandia Crest. A popular tramway, a highway, and hiking trails all climb to the crest from the city.

Right: A pool of rainwater caps the Sandstone Bluffs at El Malpais National Monument. The bluffs give a dramatic view of the *malpais,* or "badlands," that formed from lava flows only a few thousand years ago.

Far right: A summer thunderstorm provides a rainbow over grasslands at the foot of the Sacramento Mountains near Carrizozo. This area of Lincoln County was once the haunt of Billy the Kid.

Left: A shallow salt lake fills a depression in the plains southeast of Carlsbad. Potash, a type of salt, has been mined from the area for many years.

Below: The Very Large Array (VLA) radio telescope is the largest and most powerful such instrument in the world. It was built on the Plains of San Agustin because of the area's remoteness and high elevation. Astronomers use it to study objects as far away as ten billion light years.

Right: The government established Fort Selden in 1865 in the lower part of the Rio Grande Valley to protect travelers and settlers from attacks by Apaches. General Douglas MacArthur spent part of his youth at the fort when his father was stationed there in the late 1800s.

Below: The Nature Conservancy operates Bear Mountain Lodge in the foothills of the Pinos Altos Range near Silver City. The lodge's profits help fund land preservation.

Left: Aspens line the road in Santa Barbara Canyon in the Carson National Forest. The Sangre de Cristo Mountains tower above, with peaks higher than 13,000 feet.

Below: Pumpkins, squash, and cornstalks mark autumn at the Martinez Hacienda in Taos. Construction on the large adobe building began in 1804; its 21 rooms surrounding 2 courtyards have been restored to their colonial appearance and are open to tours.

Right: Dilapidated buildings dot the hills in Mogollon, an old mining town located high in the Mogollon Range in southwestern New Mexico. Once a rowdy mining camp full of saloons with names such as the Bloated Goat, it died after the mines folded. In recent years a few hardy new residents have brought the small town back to life.

Facing page: A paved trail winds down into the entrance of Carlsbad Cavern, ultimately reaching a depth of 829 feet. The cave holds one of the world's largest chambers, with an area of 14 acres and a ceiling height of 255 feet. Beautiful formations adorn the cave's walls, floors, and ceilings.

Right: Sandhill cranes wade in a marsh at Bosque del Apache National Wildlife Refuge on a winter sunrise. Many thousands of sandhill cranes, snow geese, Canada geese, ducks, and other birds winter here every year.

Below: At Chaco Culture National Historical Park, the ruins of Pueblo Bonito lie at the foot of towering sandstone cliffs. The massive ruin once had more than 600 rooms and 40 kivas. Chaco was a major center of Anasazi culture in the Southwest from about 900 to 1200.

Right: The last rays of the sun highlight the ruins of the church and pueblo at Gran Quivira in Salinas Pueblo Missions National Monument. Spaniards established a mission there in 1629, but it was abandoned about 40 years later because of drought, famine, disease, and Apache and Comanche raids.

Left: *Farolitos,* bright luminaries, decorate the walls of the unique Inn at Loretto in Santa Fe during the Christmas season. Its architecture is modeled after that of historic Taos Pueblo.

Below: Over thousands of years, dripping water carrying calcium carbonate has created beautiful formations in the Papoose Room of Carlsbad Cavern.

Right: The Rio Grande Gorge Bridge was built in 1965 just west of Taos. The bridge rises 600 feet above the river and was the second highest in the world when it was constructed.

Below: White Sands National Monument contains part of a vast 275-square-mile sea of gypsum dunes, the largest of its type in the world. The gypsum was eroded out of surrounding mountains, formed crystals in shallow lakes in the valley bottom, and then was eroded into wind-blown sand grains.

The vast Plains of San Agustin, at about 7,000 feet, are a large valley ringed by high mountains in southwestern New Mexico.

Left: Erosion has carved fanciful shapes from soft layers of sandstone, shale, and clay in the Bisti Badlands south of Farmington. Wilderness designation protects the stark desert landscape from future development.

Below: Craft sale in Old Town Albuquerque. KERRICK JAMES

Right: Cottonwoods line the banks of the Chama River near Abiquiu in fall. The river rises just north of Chama in Colorado and flows south to join the Rio Grande near Española.

Below: Big Hatchet Peak rises above a windmill in far southwestern New Mexico, in part of the state known as the Bootheel.

Left: Snow blankets the craggy heights of the Organ Mountains near Las Cruces in winter. The mountains are popular with hikers and rock climbers.

Below: Marmots thrive in the harsh climate at and above timberline in the Sangre de Cristo Mountains. Hikers often see the friendly creatures in high-elevation sections of the Pecos and Wheeler Peak wildernesses.

Right: The Santuario de Chimayó was built as a family chapel by Bernardo Abeyta between 1813 and 1816. The site is popular with both tourists and people coming to get a sample of the chapel's sacred earth, reputed for its healing powers.

Below: Thousands of petroglyphs dot the basalt rocks of West Mesa at Petroglyph National Monument.

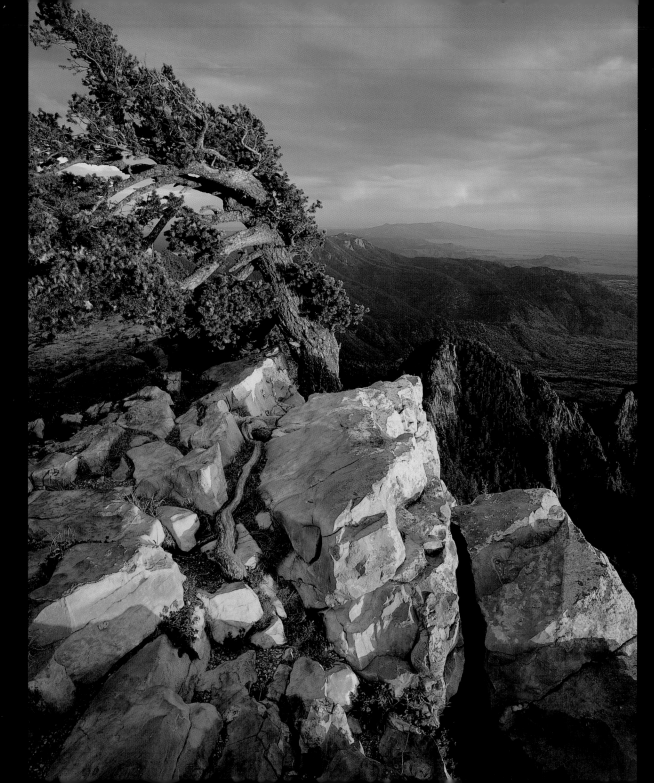

A windswept Douglas-fir clings to the rim of Sandia Crest. The crest marks the high point of the Sandia Mountains, one of several ranges within the Cibola National Forest.

Fort Union was built in 1851 to protect travelers on the Santa Fe Trail and area settlers from Indian attacks. It was abandoned in 1891 after the threat ended and was later designated a national monument.

Above: A lone cottonwood stands in a grassy field in the lower Mimbres Valley, an area first occupied by the Mimbres Indians.

Right: A rainbow arches over high desert grasslands at the foot of Bear Mountain in the Gila National Forest.

Left: Rich grasslands cover the mountain foothills near Mule Creek, a tiny ranching settlement northwest of Silver City.

Below: Legend has it that a UFO with aliens crashed near Roswell in 1947 and was subsequently covered up by the military. The city makes the most of the incident and even has a UFO museum and festival.

Above: Aspens in vibrant fall color grace the slopes of the Sangre de Cristo Mountains high above Santa Fe in the Santa Fe National Forest.

Right: Adobe ruins are all that remain of once-bustling Fort Union. It was built along the Santa Fe Trail near Las Vegas to protect settlers and travelers after the state was acquired from Mexico in the Treaty of Guadalupe Hidalgo at the end of the Mexican-American War.

Above: Other than a few stone ruins, little remains of Elizabethtown. The town, located between Eagle Nest and Red River, boomed after gold was discovered in the surrounding mountains in 1866.

Left: A reconstructed kiva, a Pueblo Indian ceremonial chamber, lies along the Rio Grande below the Sandia Mountains near Bernalillo in Coronado State Monument. The kiva was part of Kuaua Pueblo, a site occupied by Tiwa Indians from about 1300 to 1600.

Left: The South Fork of Bonito Creek tumbles down through lush forest in the White Mountain Wilderness. Popular hiking trails criss-cross the high mountain wilderness in the Lincoln National Forest near Ruidoso.

Below: Porcupines are found throughout much of the state. The sharp-quilled animals often eat the bark of piñon pines and other trees.

Above: Skiing the deep powder at Taos Ski Valley. RANKIN HARVEY/HOUSERSTOCK

Right: Snow blankets the sagebrush-covered valley below the Sangre de Cristo Mountains near Questa.

Above: Dozens of brilliantly colored balloons thrill spectators in a mass ascension at Albuquerque's annual Balloon Fiesta. KERRICK JAMES

Left: The Santa Fe Southern Railway offers train trips year round between central Santa Fe and the tiny village of Lamy on the Atchison, Topeka and Santa Fe Railroad's main line.

Left: Santa Fe is famous worldwide for its adobe-style architecture. The oldest state capital in the United States, the city is nestled in the Sangre de Cristo foothills at an elevation of 7,000 feet.

Below: The Rio Grande roars out of Colorado, running high with snowmelt. The river has cut a deep gorge near Taos that is popular with river rafters. Some trips pass under the high Rio Grande Gorge Bridge. PATRICIA CAPERTON PARENT

Right: Inscription Rock records the carvings made by passing travelers over hundreds of years. Indians started the practice with their petroglyphs. Juan de Oñate, the founder of the first Spanish settlement in New Mexico, left his mark in 1605, and many other carvings followed at El Morro National Monument.

Below: A large desert spring in the foothills of the Guadalupe Mountains feeds a lush corridor of vegetation and spills over a cliff, creating 100-foot-high Sitting Bull Falls. The falls are a popular attraction in summer in the Lincoln National Forest.

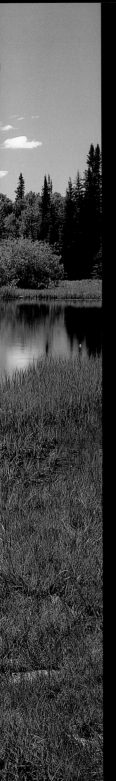

Left: The small Canjilon Lakes lie at over 10,000 feet in the Tusas Mountains near Chama. Much of the range, an extension of the San Juan Mountains of Colorado, falls within the Carson National Forest.

Below: Black bears are relatively common in the higher mountains of New Mexico. This bear was photographed in the Manzano Mountains southeast of Albuquerque.

Right: Although much of New Mexico is desert, rushing mountain streams such as this one in the Wheeler Peak Wilderness near Taos tumble down from many of the state's highest mountains.

Far right: Tranquil Nambe Lake is one of many natural glacier-formed alpine lakes found in the Pecos Wilderness. The 223,000-acre wilderness contains the headwaters of the Pecos River and snow-capped peaks that reach over 13,000 feet.

Below: Capulin Volcano, part of a massive volcanic field, rises to 8,182 feet from the high, grassy plains of northeastern New Mexico. The centerpiece of Capulin Volcano National Monument, it erupted as recently as about 59,000 years ago.

Left: A fire burned more than 50,000 acres of the Black Range high country in the early 1950s, but aspens have reforested it, creating beautiful fall color displays. The Gila National Forest manages most of the mountains, including this spot in the Aldo Leopold Wilderness.

Far left: Private owners protect the remnants of the old mining town of Shakespeare near Lordsburg. The owners offer tours to visitors wanting to see the old ghost town. At least 15 saloons served the town during its prime.

Above: This classic adobe church lies in Las Trampas, a tiny village along the High Road between Santa Fe and Taos. The village was settled in 1751 by twelve Santa Fe families.

Facing page: Hungo Pavi is one of several great house ruins at Chaco Culture National Historical Park. Construction of the massive structures began in the tenth century. Archaeologists believe that Chaco was the center of Anasazi civilization in the San Juan Basin for many years. The area was abandoned by 1300.

Left: Fresh snow blankets the Pinos Altos Range near Silver City.

Below: Ship Rock rises above the Navajo Reservation in northwestern New Mexico. It is a volcanic neck formed when overlying softer rocks eroded away, leaving only the harder rock from the throat of the volcano.

Left: A simple stone obelisk marks the world's first nuclear test at Trinity Site. On July 16, 1945, the bomb was exploded before dawn, ushering in the nuclear age.

Below: The great kiva at Aztec Ruins National Monument is the largest reconstructed kiva in the Southwest. The kiva and related pueblos were built in the early 1100s and were tied to the culture at Chaco Canyon.

Right: This helicopter is part of the Vietnam Veterans National Memorial near Eagle Nest. It was constructed through the efforts of the Victor Westphall family. The chapel, built in 1971, was the first memorial honoring Vietnam veterans in the United States.

Far right: The Cumbres and Toltec Scenic Railroad carries passengers from Chama over 10,015-foot Cumbres Pass into Colorado. The narrow-gauge railroad was built in 1881 to connect Denver and other eastern cities to the rich mines of the San Juan Mountains around Durango and Silverton, Colorado.

Above: Dave McGary's sculpture "Free Spirits at Noisy Water" marks the entrance to the Hubbard Museum of the American West. The Ruidoso museum houses an outstanding collection of Western fine art, carriages, saddles, wagons, Indian artifacts, and other items. PATRICIA CAPERTON PARENT

Above: Frijoles Creek flows through the heart of Bandelier National Monument and over two waterfalls, including Upper Falls. The creek's permanent waters allowed the settlement of Bandelier by Pueblo Indians from the early 1100s to abandonment in the early 1500s.

Left: A kiva has been reconstructed in Ceremonial Cave at Bandelier National Monument. A series of tall ladders allows visitors to climb up to the cave and its ruins.

Right: The Jackalope in Santa Fe has a huge selection of Southwestern items for sale.

Below: Cars aren't the only way to visit the Burger King restaurant in Taos.

Above: The adobe church ruin is the most prominent remnant of the once thriving pueblo and Spanish mission at Pecos National Historical Park. The pueblo, constructed in the ninth century, was at its peak of importance and size in 1540 when Coronado visited. It became a Spanish mission in the 1600s, but was abandoned in 1838.

Left: Mount Taylor looms over the Sandstone Bluffs of El Malpais National Monument at sunset on a winter evening. Eruptions beginning four million years ago created the 11,301-foot volcano over the course of two million years.

LAURENCE PARENT

Laurence Parent was born and raised in New Mexico. After receiving a petroleum engineering degree at the University of Texas at Austin, he practiced engineering for six years before becoming a full-time freelance photographer and writer specializing in landscape, travel, and nature subjects. He was drawn to the profession by a love of the outdoors and a desire to work for himself. His photos appear in many calendars and in magazines such as *National Geographic Traveler, Men's Journal, Outside, Newsweek, Arizona Highways, Travel & Leisure,* and *New Mexico Magazine.* He has had 27 books published. Commercial clients include Southwest Airlines, Temple-Inland, Compass Banks, and Cox Enterprises. He makes his home near Austin, Texas, with his wife Patricia and two children.